PHONES DOWN, PLEASE!

Written by Mark Jovic

Illustrated by Diana O'Brien

GP's Honey Tomes, LLC
New York

Published by GP's Honey Tomes, LLC,
P.O. Box 164, Bronx, New York 10464
GPhoneytomes@yahoo.com.

ISBN: 978-0-9968765-9-9
Graphic Design/Illustration: Diana O'Brien
Printing: Country Pines Printing, Indiana

Printed in the United States

Especially For

Camila

With Love

Daddy

To my daughter, who has filled my heart
with the footprint of creation itself

Please put down your phone, Mommy.

Would you like to see what I see?

Will you play with me?

Let's get Mommy.
Quick!
Sneak through the woods. We will trap her.
We have you now, Mommy.
You have nowhere to run.
Give up now.

Look, Daddy. Can you see what I see?

Time is running out.

Please put down your phone and play with me.

Oh no, Dad!
Watch out!
The giant bird is coming.
I will protect you! Silly Daddy.
The monster bird almost ate you.
Please put down your phone
and play with me.

Mommy, Daddy, do you see what I see?

Look! Look! Look!

Please put down your phones and play with me.

The parade is passing you by.
We still have time.
If only you would put
down your phones
and play with me...

Mom said there are no sea monsters in the pool.
Dad said there are no dinosaurs in there, either.
Are they confused?
If they could just see what we see...

Do you want to see what I see? It's right here.
You just have to put down your phones and play with me.
Then you can see what I see.
You can see all the magic that I see.

Wow, Grandma. Look!

Did you ever see anything like this?

If only Mom would put down her phone and play with me...

Yes, honey. A long, long time ago,
I found a beast. It tried to eat me,
but your Mommy saved me.
Then, she could see.
She used to see what we can see.

Look, Daddy.
There is still time to see the magic,
but it does not stay long.

Hurry! Hurry!

It is still here to see if you put down your
phone and play with me...

Hi, Mr. Train! How are you?
          Good. Verrry goooood!
Where are you going?

Well, of course, to take you over the pink
mountains to the forest of unicorns.
Hurry! Hurry! There is still time
to see all the magic.

Sometimes it makes me feel so **sad**
that Mommy and Daddy don't see me.
If only they would put down their phones
and play with me...

Don't worry, my child.
Mommy and Daddy can see.
They still have time.
Tomorrow can be different.
Their eyes can open.
The time for magic is short,
but once they play, they will see.

Yes, Mommy. Yes, Daddy.
Your eyes are open.
You now can see all the magic.
You will remember at the end how you played with me.
Now that you have put down your phones, we can be a family.

About the Author

Mark Jovic was born in Flushing, Queens and grew up on Long Island where he resides with his wife and daughter. The son of immigrant parents from Croatia, Mark has a BA in Psychology and a BS in Nursing.

For enjoyment, Mark is an avid fisherman, having learned to fish at a very young age from his grandfather and father. He loves to drive his mom and wife crazy with his passion for cars and motorcycles. The remainder of his time is spent in the mythical land of Otariac with his beloved daughter. Together, they sail its vast seas, tame dragons, and call lightning from the heavens. Much to their disappointment, they are reminded by his lovely wife each Monday that school and work await them and so off they go until their next adventure.

About the Illustrator

Diana O'Brien was born and raised on Long Island, where she lives with her husband and daughter. She is a graphic designer and illustrator with a diverse career path. She has an AAS in Advertising Design, BS in Visual Communications, and is working on an MFA in Illustration.

Diana likes to create imaginary worlds using her old-fashioned pencils, paint, and digital art supplies. She has painted murals in children's hospitals across the country, designed brochures and presentations, and filled sketchbooks and composition notebooks with her experience. She's traveled over a vast range of metaphorical mountains to get to her husband, John, and daughter, Grace, where she finds (relative) peace, hope and inspiration.

www.dianaobrienart.com